The Cookie House

Modern Curriculum Press
BEGINNING
TO
READ
Series

The COOKIE HOUSE

Margaret Hillert

Illustrated by Kinuko Craft

MODERN CURRICULUM PRESS
Cleveland • Toronto

ISBN 0-8136-5512-9   Paperback
ISBN 0-8136-5012-7   Hardbound

11 12 13 14 15 16 17 18 19 20   02 01 00 99 98 97

5

Get up. Get up.
Come with us.
We will go to work.

6

Oh, this is fun.
We can run and jump.
We like it here.

You two play here.
You do not have to work.
We will go now.
But we will come back to get you.

Look here.
Here is something for us.
Something we like.
Have one.

10

And here is something.
It is little.
It can play with us.

Mother is not here.
Father is not here.
I do not like this.

We can not find the way.

What can we do now?

Who will help us?

I want to go.

We can not go now.
Come down here with me.
Come down, down, down.

Get up. Get up.
Look what I see.
Can you see it, too?
Look up, up.

Look at it go.
We can go, too.
Run, run, run.

Oh, see the little house.
I like it.
I like it.
What fun for us.

Look at this and this and this.

I want one.

You can have one, too.

No, you can not.
You can not have that.
It is not for you.

20

Oh, help, help.
I do not like it in here.
Help me.
Help me.

Here I come.
I will help you.
See me help.

Go in. Go in.
We do not like you.
I will make you go in.
In you go.

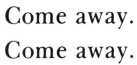

Come away.

Come away.

24

Here we go.
Run, run, run.

What is this?
What can we do now?
We can not go in here.

Oh, look at us.
What fun.
What a ride this is!

I see Father.
Father, Father.
Here we are, Father.

28

The Cookie House

Uses of This Book: Reading for fun. This easy-to-read retelling of Hansel and Gretel is sure to excite the rich imaginations of children.

Word List
All of the 59 words used in *The Cookie House* are listed. Numbers refer to the page on which each word first appears.

6	get		run	**10**	look	**14**	down
	up		and		something		me
	come		jump		for	**15**	see
	with		like		one		too
	us		it	**11**	little	**16**	at
	we		here	**12**	mother	**17**	house
	will	**9**	you		father	**20**	no
	go		two		I		that
	to		play	**13**	find	**21**	in
	work		do		the	**23**	make
8	oh		not		way	**24**	away
	this		have		what	**27**	a
	is		now		who		ride
	fun		but		help	**28**	are
	can		back		want		